CINCO DE MAYO

By EMMA CARLSON BERNE
Illustrations by GERALDINE RODRÍGUEZ
Music by MARK OBLINGER

CANTATA
LEARNING

WWW.CANTATALEARNING.COM

Published by Cantata Learning
1710 Roe Crest Drive
North Mankato, MN 56003
www.cantatalearning.com

Library of Congress Cataloging-in-Publication Data
Names: Berne, Emma Carlson, author.
Title: Cinco de Mayo / by Emma Carlson Berne ; illustrations by Geraldine Rodríguez ; music by Mark Oblinger.
Description: North Mankato, MN : Cantata Learning, [2018] | Series: Holidays in rhythm and rhyme | Audience: Grades K-3. | Audience: Ages 5-7.
Identifiers: LCCN 2017017502 (print) | LCCN 2017018282 (ebook) | ISBN 9781684101511 (ebook) | ISBN 9781684101153 (hardcover : alk. paper) | ISBN 9781684101900 (pbk. : alk. paper)
Subjects: LCSH: Cinco de Mayo (Mexican holiday)--History--Juvenile literature. | Mexico--Social life and customs--Juvenile literature. | Mexican Americans--Social life and customs--Juvenile literature. |Puebla, Battle of, Puebla de Zaragoza, Mexico, 1862--Juvenile literature.
Classification: LCC F1233 (ebook) | LCC F1233 .B45 2018 (print) | DDC 394.262--dc23
LC record available at https://lccn.loc.gov/2017017502

978-1-68410-397-3 (hardcover)

Book design and art direction, Tim Palin Creative
Editorial direction, Kellie M. Hultgren
Music direction, Elizabeth Draper
Music arranged and produced by Mark Oblinger

Printed in the United States 6331

TIPS TO SUPPORT LITERACY AT HOME

WHY READING AND SINGING WITH YOUR CHILD IS SO IMPORTANT

Daily reading with your child leads to increased academic achievement. Music and songs, specifically rhyming songs, are a fun and easy way to build early literacy and language development. Music skills correlate significantly with both phonological awareness and reading development. Singing helps build vocabulary and speech development. And reading and appreciating music together is a wonderful way to strengthen your relationship.

READ AND SING EVERY DAY!

TIPS FOR USING CANTATA LEARNING BOOKS AND SONGS DURING YOUR DAILY STORY TIME

1. As you sing and read, point out the different words on the page that rhyme. Suggest other words that rhyme.
2. Memorize simple rhymes such as Itsy Bitsy Spider and sing them together. This encourages comprehension skills and early literacy skills.
3. Use the questions in the back of each book to guide your singing and storytelling.
4. Read the included sheet music with your child while you listen to the song. How do the music notes correlate to the words of the song?
5. Sing along on the go and at home. Access music by scanning the QR code on each Cantata book, or by using the included CD. You can also stream or download the music for free to your computer, smartphone, or mobile device.

Devoting time to daily reading shows that you are available for your child. Together, you are building language, literacy, and listening skills.

Have fun reading and singing!

Cinco de Mayo means "Fifth of May" in Spanish. This holiday **celebrates** a big battle that happened on May 5, 1862. The army of Mexico was fighting the army of France. Everyone thought the army of France would win. But the army of Mexico fought hard. They won the battle. People were very happy and surprised.

On Cinco de Mayo, people remember that battle. They also celebrate Mexican American **culture**. They eat Mexican food. They play Mexican music. They dance Mexican dances.

Let's sing about Cinco de Mayo together!

On the fifth of May, we fly the flag
that's colored green, red, and white.

We remember Mexico's army
and their brave, long-ago fight.

HISTORIA
DE
MÉXICO

Let's dance a dance, let's play a song.

It's Cinco de Mayo today!

Let's eat the food of Mexico,

pozole, **tortillas**–hooray!

The music of Mexico fills our ears,
maracas and strumming guitars.

This band is called **mariachi**, and they play for us under the stars.

Let's dance a dance, let's play a song.

It's Cinco de Mayo today!

Let's eat the food of Mexico,
pozole, *tortillas*–hooray!

Cut tomatillos for *salsa verde*,

and slice up the meat for *carne asada*.

Grilled corn on the cob is called *elote*.

Now we just need the *enchiladas*!

Let's dance a dance, let's play a song.
It's Cinco de Mayo today!

Let's eat the food of Mexico,
pozole, *tortillas*–hooray!

Come learn the Mexican Hat Dance!

Find a partner, stand up tall.

Get ready to tap your feet
as the trumpets play for us all.

Let's dance a dance, let's play a song.
It's Cinco de Mayo today!

Let's eat the food of Mexico,
pozole, tortillas–hooray!

SONG LYRICS

Cinco de Mayo

On the fifth of May, we fly the flag
that's colored green, red, and white.
We remember Mexico's army
and their brave, long-ago fight.

Let's dance a dance, let's play a song.
It's Cinco de Mayo today!
Let's eat the food of Mexico,
pozole, tortillas–hooray!

The music of Mexico fills our ears,
maracas and strumming guitars.
This band is called mariachi,
and they play for us under the stars.

Let's dance a dance, let's play a song.
It's Cinco de Mayo today!
Let's eat the food of Mexico,
pozole, tortillas–hooray!

Cut tomatillos for *salsa verde*,
and slice up the meat for *carne asada*.
Grilled corn on the cob is called *elote*.
Now we just need the *enchiladas*!

Let's dance a dance, let's play a song.
It's Cinco de Mayo today!
Let's eat the food of Mexico,
pozole, tortillas–hooray!

Come learn the Mexican Hat Dance!
Find a partner, stand up tall.
Get ready to tap your feet
as the trumpets play for us all.

Let's dance a dance, let's play a song,
It's Cinco de Mayo today!
Let's eat the food of Mexico,
pozole, tortillas–hooray!

Cinco de Mayo

Holiday/Mariachi
Mark Oblinger

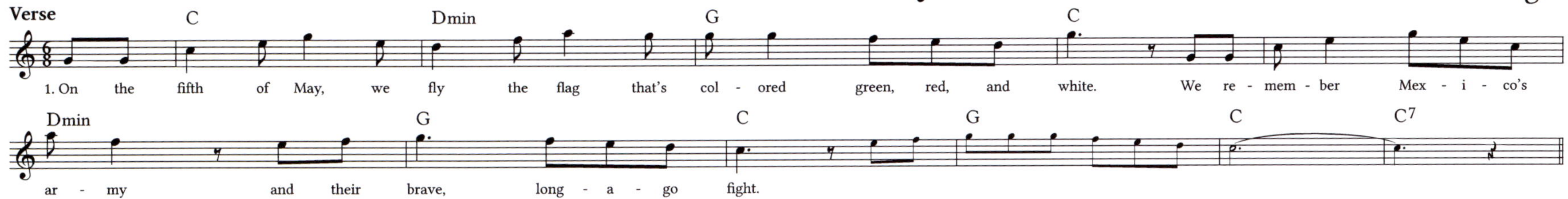

Verse 2
The music of Mexico fills our ears,
maracas and strumming guitars.
This band is called mariachi,
and they play for us under the stars.

Chorus

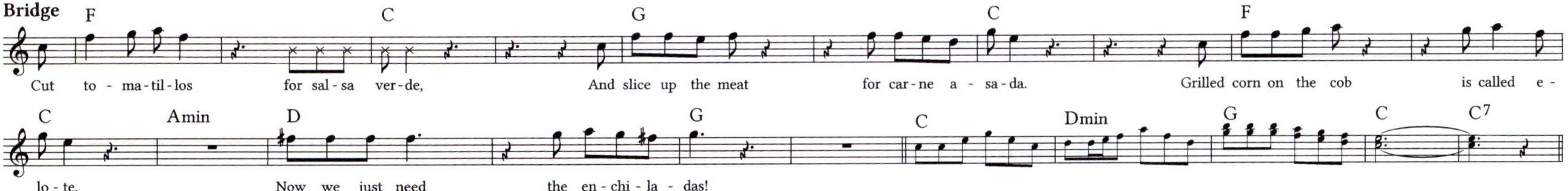

Chorus

Verse 3
Come learn the Mexican Hat Dance!
Find a partner, stand up tall.
Get ready to tap your feet
as the trumpets play for us all.

Chorus

GLOSSARY

celebrate—to do activities to mark a special, happy time

culture—the food people eat, the clothes they wear, the music they listen to. These things make people who they are.

maracas—traditional Mexican musical shakers

mariachi—a type of traditional Mexican band that includes a guitar, a horn, and a violin

pozole—a type of thick stew made with corn kernels

tortillas—flat, thin bread made from flour or cornmeal

GUIDED READING ACTIVITIES

1. Cinco de Mayo remembers the day of a great battle. The Mexican army was very brave. Why is it important to be brave? Can you remember a time when you were brave like the Mexican army?

2. Has your school or community ever held a Cinco de Mayo party? What were some activities you did? If not, imagine your own Cinco de Mayo party. Draw a picture of how you would celebrate.

3. Everyone can celebrate Cinco de Mayo, even people whose families aren't Mexican American. Why is important to celebrate everyone's culture?

TO LEARN MORE

Bullard, Lisa. *Marco's Cinco de Mayo*. Minneapolis: Millbrook, 2012.

Gleisner, Jenna Lee. *We Celebrate Cinco de Mayo in Spring*. North Mankato, MN: Cherry Lake, 2014.

Smith, Maximilian. *The Story of Cinco de Mayo*. New York: Gareth Stevens, 2016.